Damaged by the World and Wounded by the Church

By:

Apostle Dr. William D. Lee

(Note from a friend of William Lee)

While helping Apostle Lee on this book, I started out thinking I would just hurry up and get it done, but, I began to read and it dawned on me that I could not pass up even one word.

I was so engrossed in the words, the meaning of the words that it amazed me!

This is a wonderful book!

I recommend that when you read this book, that you make sure you have nothing else to do...

Dedication

This book is dedicated to some wonderful people. First and foremost, Pastor Shirley Had id, who took upon herself to raise her sister's six children. I love her for believing in me when no one else would. Thank you for the many trips back and forth to the clinics and in and out of the DePaul Mental Clinic.

To my lovely wife, Pastor Telephia Lee, who stuck by me. To my wonderful children.

I am who I am today because of my uncle, Bishop Richard C. Williams, who mentored and poured the word of God in me. Thank you for not compromising the word of God with me.

To the Pastors and Churches that are under my covering, thank you for believing in me.

Introduction

In 2001 I was inspired to write this book about my life. I believe this book will encourage, heal, deliver and bring change to those who read this book. The challenges in my life were full of pain, chaos and confusion.

I was born to the late, Ann Marie Lee and to the late William D. Lee, II. I was born premature with a heart murmur and schizophrenic traces. Because of these conditions and circumstances, I was labeled emotionally disturbed by Disability and the state school system.

I met my father for the very first time at a young age, unfortunately he died shortly afterward. I was molested several times by men and women. This caused a great confusion in my life, to not love myself. I walked around feeling rejected. This brought about several attempts of suicide, but, by the grace of almighty God, I am still here today to write this book.

The devil used the constant attacks of not being accepted by people and Christians to try to destroy me. He used my past to try to ruin my future. It's funny! I didn't even know I had a future. Why would God use someone that was labeled emotionally disturbed, handicapped, and rejected by society, family and friends? I could not read, I could not write, I had a speech impediment, and all of my life people have told me over and over again that I would not amount to *anything*.

Now though, God has made me a Chief Apostle with the ability to go into any city and start a ministry and in less than thirty days, have well over one hundred members.

He took my past to create history to every non-believer. God hid me, like he hid Moses, because he did not want me to be *gifted* and not *anointed.* The hurt of not having a father-figure in my life has brought much pain.

I know that this book will encourage and bring healing to those of you that have been wounded from the inside out. I pray that reconciliation will start first with you, and second with God. Until you are healed within yourself, you can never receive *Him.*

This book, "Damaged by the World and Wounded by the Church", came through a life of pain, rejection and hurt. Can you imagine being born emotionally disturbed with high schizophrenic traces and born with a heart murmur? Due to these conditions, the ratio of being accepted by people and society is zero. Who wants to deal with someone with these types of illnesses?

The devil tried attacking my mother to get to me in the womb, because he saw the hand of God upon my life in the womb.

The devil's job is to create adversity, especially when he knows that you are going to be anointed. He watches, plots, and sets his traps by any means necessary, to attack the seed that was planted in you, even before it starts growing.

The devils job was to destroy me; But God is the Master Planner. I was destined to die, but I was chosen to live.

The devil thought that if he could kill my parents, that there would be no reason for me to live. So, that's why he started in my mother's womb, like Esau and Jacob, two nations fighting in their mother's womb. He wanted to destroy the nation that God is building in me.

At the age of six years old, after meeting my father for the first time, a week later, he died. Can you imagine that?

I'm already wounded... no father, no mother, and I am having these crazy dreams of preaching to millions of people.

I could not read, I could not write, but I could read and understand the bible.

People would call me retarded and stupid. *I would wish bad things to happen to them and it would happen.* I had a gift and did not know it.

I was molested several times for many years, by men and women.

Fear gripped me and I would never tell my aunt, the woman who had raised me, in fear that she would not believe me.

I walked in fear, and I never told anyone about the things that happened to me.

I was confused and did not know if I wanted to be a man or a woman.

I was a little boy trapped inside of a forbidden realm all by myself and I felt that no one could reach me.

I tried, relentlessly, over and over again, to befriend people; but because of my condition, I was not accepted.

The devil was not going to stop until I was dead. I tried several times to commit suicide and overdose on pills because of the pain I lived in emotionally and mentally, daily.

When I was sixteen years old, I overdosed on crack cocaine… I wanted to die, but a voice kept telling me, **"You'll live"**. The voice said, **"Not only will you live, but you will never taste death."**

As the bible informs us that *we shall not all sleep, but some shall be alive and remain when he comes. (I Cor. 15:51).*

I turned to the streets for love, and I lived a life of violence, drugs, gang banging, shooting, robbing, yet going to church.

However, the church was not in me.

At the age of twelve years old, I was called to preach. I ran because I did not understand what I was feeling and what I was seeing. I could look at people and their whole life would flash before me.

Wow! Can you imagine seeing them but not seeing yourself?

I finally gave my life to the Lord.

At the age of twelve, I started preaching.

The devil did not let up with his attacks.

I was in and out of church; and back to my drug selling and smoking.

When you've got drugs, you've got power!

I had six prostitutes working for me at the age of sixteen. I didn't know about life, but the devil made sure that I was exposed to it.

He wanted to stop the mandate on my life, so he was giving me temporary fixes for a permanent condition.

I ran from God, as long as I could, but was stopped by getting shot point blank, in the head, with a nine millimeter hand gun.

The devil thought that I was dead on the scene.

That night God took his blood and put it in my veins and spared me. Every life changing event that I have dealt with in my past has brought this book up to speed today.

It has now been twenty nine years that I've been in the ministry. Out of those twenty nine years, I have only been sold out- about eight of those years.

The reason I am anointed is because of my confession.

I have no hidden sins or agendas.

Any and everything that I have ever dealt with in my life, I have shared it with my parishioners.

I want you to know, that because I am a Pastor, does not mean that I am exempt from mistakes. I have made a lot of errors and bad decisions because I had no one that was willing to father me. They either became jealous, or maybe I did not fit in their click because I refused to be like them.

All I've ever wanted was for someone to show some type of interest in my life. I wanted to be accepted in a relationship, friendship or even marriage. It was hard, because I refused to believe in myself because of what *they* said I was.

I came up under strict *church rules,* where everything was a sin.

It was a sin if you wore make up, big earrings, if your dress was too short, and being a man I could not wear tank tops because I was revealing too much. *Everything* was a *sin.*

This book is for those that have been violated by the world and the church, looking for a means of direction and support.

The thing that I don't understand is that we are so caught up in the "Organization" that we don't know about the organism; which is the body of Christ.

Many are gifted, but where is the anointing?

It's time that we separate church and state.

The church has gone wild.

Any and everything is accepted as long as you are a good tithe payer.

You can dress like you want, sin like you want, and come if you want. The church has become lackadaisical.

Certain things that would not be tolerated are now being tolerated just to fill a position.

Homosexuals and Lesbians are holding positions in the church such as Pastors, Apostles and Bishops. For the bible says, *(Rom 1:26) For this cause God gave them up to vile affections, for even their women did change their natural use into that which is against nature and likewise also the men leaving the natural use of the woman burned in their lust one toward another. Men with men working that which is unseeingly. And receiving within themselves the recompense of their error which was meeting.*

The church is out of position because many failed to hook up with Judah, which means praise.

Where is the worship and deliverance?

I believe in the "whole" bible...

I preach the "whole" bible from Genesis to Revelation without compromise.

Guess what? When it's bringing so much controversy, that's when you know you are Christ like!

In some aspects, the bible is being misinterpreted.

Here's a familiar scripture, *A good name is better than riches, (Prov. 22:1).*

So we think it applies to the church. It doesn't.

It is impossible to have a good name in the church. For the bible says that *if any man lives godly he MUST suffer persecution.* That messes your good name up.

We are counted all the day long like sheep to the slaughter.

The bible also says "beware of every man that speaks well of you".

Jesus never had a good name.

He was smitten and stricken of men.

Lied on every day.

Talked about every day, but he opened not his mouth.

 Many churches have allowed politics and money to become their main source instead of Jehovah Jireh, your provider.

I have lacked much in ministry, I have desired to have a spiritual father or mother, to seek their wisdom, to stand with me as I build the Kingdom of God, but the more I sought for a man or woman to be a spiritual parent, my pains increased of disappointments and hurts because as a Prophet I would see their heart's intent to deceive me into believing they were with me, but plotting to take from me.

Many have even used these words "God did not call you"! You are not anointed!"

Many saw the gift and wanted to prostitute my gift!

They wanted to be around only the gift, but refuse to help me, by killing me with my past.

Many I tried to connect with refused to open doors for me because they desired to have the mantle I possessed, not realizing God did this... I did not do this of my own will.

These pains in ministry cause me many times to want to run into seclusion.

My paths have crossed with those in ministry who would use my past mistakes in the church and as a child to gain credibility and notoriety among the people.

To pull my name down and raise theirs up.

This was done on a number of occasions.

Each time as I suffered in these paths, my words would be "I can't help that I'm anointed"!

I would get angry with God, because I didn't understand why he would keep allowing people to wound and hurt me. I told God "Haven't I suffered enough from my childhood?" His reply, **"I'm doing it for your good. I'm using your suffering and your trials to reposition you."**!

If you are one of these people that are going through what I have been through, let me encourage you. It's not going to stop; He'll just give you the strength to endure it.

For the bible says, *he that endures to the end, shall be saved.*

The problem we are facing is not from the world, it's from the church. When are we going to stop thinking that we are better than each other, more anointed than each other?

We get favor caught up with schemes and tricks.

Because you have a mega ministry does not mean God is with you. Your storefront church does not mean that He sent you. Let me introduce you to a real Christian. The word Christian means to be Christ like. The bible says, that Charity *suffer long and it is kind, charity envieth not, Charity vaunted not itself, is not puffed up, does not behave itself unseeingly, seeking not her own, is not easily provoked, thinketh no evil, rejoiceth not in iniquity but rejoiceth in truth, bearers all things, believeth all things, hope all things, endureth all things. (I Cor. 13:4)*

So tell me, what in the world is wrong with this church?

I am not otherwise convinced that this is not the church that he died for. If this was the church he died for, why is he judging it first?

What we call church today, is a joke!

Many are operating out of flesh.

Many use the church for a battleground to crush people that are already wounded by constantly revealing their past to other preachers and Christians.

I thought the bible said, ye that are spiritual restore such a one in a spirit of meekness. Considering yourself.

Where has the church gone wrong?

If you are a Pastor or fall under the category of a preacher, you must understand that God wants *His* church back.

Many have adopted their own ways, but it's either God's way or no way at all.

Does it not frighten you that he is judging the church first?

I don't blame the sheep, I blame the preachers.

Let's analyze this for a second.

Preachers and Pastors are two different people.

He never called them preachers, but he called them Pastors.

The bible says *I will give you pastors after my heart which will feed you. (Jer. 3:15)*

I preached a message, "The Blood has a Voice".

The blood of God's people is crying out from the church to be free from these modern day Pharaoh's.

They operate out of a spirit of Control, which has now become best friends with a Leviathan spirit.

The reason God spoke to Moses to tell Pharaoh to *"let my people go"*, is because he was tired of them being oppressed by a hard task master.

You better not be one of those who are controlling God's people!

Here is the sad scenario...after Moses freed the people; he didn't even make it in the promise land. God commanded him to go up and write the Ten Commandments, and when he returned, the church was out of control. He started putting his mouth on God's people.

God told Moses, because of what you have done, you will see the promise land but you will not enter in. Wow!

To the Pastors that are living holy and are being attacked by witchcraft and sorcery, remember that no weapon that is formed against you shall prosper.

The attack is not against you, but it is against all that you stand for.

If you don't stand for something, you're going to fall for anything.

Don't allow yourself to be swindled and drawn in with these circles and cliques. Keep your integrity and most of all, your anointing!

I pray that through this book, many are restored and enlightened. The church was meant to be a haven, a place of restoration; but many churches have become dogmatic.

You can tell who is not Christ like because Christians do not gossip.

Christians are not false accusers.

Christians are not busy bodies in other man's matters.

Most of all, Christians walk in a spirit of forgiveness and humility.

I want to apologize to every real Pastor and Christian that's being attacked by the legalism of doctrine.

Those of you who refuse to sell out to them, they won't let you in.

Don't worry about getting in.

The bible says the first shall be last, and the last shall be first.

Those that live by the gospel and are sold out to God: plan to walk alone because Jesus was alone.

People are fighting for position and they will do anything to get it.

Many are chasing man but have forgotten God.

Until you sell out to God, you will continue to join churches.

Giving the preacher your hand, but never giving God your heart.

I tried to call and encourage several TV Pastors and because I have no recognition or clout, if you will, I'm not recognized or respected.

Several big time Pastors I've tried to call, I won't mention their names, but you know them.

Scrutiny in the body, I tried to warn them:

Because they didn't know me, they wouldn't accept my calls or the word that was coming forth as a warning from the Lord.

With grief in my heart, every warning that was released from me to their assistance did not reach them.

Each and every one of them, fell.

When are we going to get to the point when we will stop thinking it's all about us?

When will we get to the point that we will begin to cover each other?

These circles in God's house are destroying the Church and turning it into a circus.

The bible says that they have their reward.

If I were you, I would give God His church back.

I've had several Pastors tell me over the years that I'm stealing members.

It is Impossible!

The bible says *"all souls are Gods"*.

Let me give you a scripture. Jeremiah 23 says *"Woe be unto the Pastors that destroy and scatter the sheep of my pasture, sayeth the Lord"*.

Whose sheep? *Therefore, thus said the Lord God of Israel against the Pastors that feed my people*.

Whose people? *"Ye have scattered my flock and driven them away"*.

Uh-Oh! That sounds like brutish Pastors to me. *"And have NOT visited them. Behold, I will visit upon you the evil of your doings, sayeth the Lord"*.

Here's an encouragement to you pastor's that have dealt with the same attack because you are anointed. *"And I will gather the remnant of my flock"*.

Whose flock? *"Out of all countries. Wither I have driven them and will bring them again to other folds and they shall be fruitful and increase. And I will set up shepherds over them"*.

Sounds like to me that he just took from you and gave to somebody else that wouldn't abuse them.

That wouldn't control them. *"And he said they shall feed them and they shall fear no more"*.

God's people are afraid to go visit another ministry.

God's people are afraid to walk in their calling.

Many **preachers walk in a spirit of Control which is not of God.**

It is witchcraft.

Asking them to give you a letter if they leave your ministry.

Your words should be "I didn't give you a letter when I joined!"

People are always going to be coming from somewhere on their way to somewhere else.

They might not have left the first church right, so when did they become our property.

I don't need people in the church to condemn me.

Many times we already feel condemned.

One of the most painful things that you can experience in life is hurt from the church.

I've been to the point where I tried to reach out to another brother, sister in Christ or pastor with what I was experiencing and dealing with, and before the cock crowed thrice it was in the street.

I guess the church is full of Peters. Betrayal should not be on your lips, but that's impossible, because it's in your heart.

I remember going into cities to do revivals.

I had to rent a hotel or a building because the Pastors would get jealous and wouldn't open their doors.

As the meetings grew and souls were delivered and demons were cast out, the assaults started.

Whispers and heresies started to try to kill the revival.

But I have news for you; you can't kill what's already dead.

I'm dead to the world!

And for you Apostles and Bishops that have tried to start ministry in different cities and came through great opposition because of your anointing, be steadfast and unmovable.

You will complete your task!

You know what's mind boggling to me?

That many believe that they own or control a certain city.

If God tells you to start a church there, they will tell you that it is not God because they fear the anointing that is in you.

We have many churches!

"But where is the anointing?"

Everybody wants to be the boss, but refuse to step down when they get up in age.

They don't want anyone else to carry the vision.

Why would you want your vision to die?

The bible says, *"that he called the young because they are strong and the old because they know the way"*.

Did you not write the vision and make it plain so that they that read it could run with it?

Why let the vision die because of control?

All of my life as a Pastor, I've been attacked by other preachers debating God's Word.

Telling me the bible doesn't mean *that.*

Throwing off and preaching on each other on National television as if they are greater than you. When in fact, the bible says *"knowing this first that no prophecy of the scripture is of any private interpretation." (2 Pet. 1:20)....* *"But there were false prophets also among the people even as there should be false teachers among you who should privily bring in damnable heresies, even denying the Lord that bought them and bring upon themselves swift destruction. And many shall follow their pernicious ways by reason of whom the word of truth shall be evil spoken of." (2 Pet. 2:1).*

As a Pastor, I also experienced fellowship with other churches that would not return the favor.

When it came time for the offering, they would tell me split the offering 50/50 and you keep the envelopes.

But when they saw that the envelopes were more than the offering, they started wanting the envelopes.

That's okay, they have their reward too.

The bible says "don't be overcome with evil but overcome evil with good".

I have had preachers fly me in, as if everything was in order.

Hotel wasn't paid for, membership was low, and I had to call home to get home.

The spirit of Control is running rapid through many Christians.

I don't know about you, but I'm tired of people using their position as a weapon.

In this day and time, many people struggle to be saved.

So, we can do without insults from the church.

The devil desires to keep us unclean, so we must separate ourselves from unclean things.

You must be careful what you watch on television.

Be careful who you hang around with and where you go.

The bible says, "come out from among them and be ye separated".

When cliques start in your church, run and don't look back!

When people call you with gossip, run and don't look back!

For the bible says, "let not this be named among you".

It took me a long time to be healed and be delivered from people.

In order for your temple to stay clean you have to resist temptation; lust, lying, backbiting.

It's hard to be saved only because we have not submitted our whole heart unto God.

You must lay aside every weight (and the sin) that so easily beset you.

You can't continue to hang around gossipers, backbiters and liars and expect to have a clean spirit.

When we are not sold out to God, we make so many excuses why we can't go to church, why we can't surrender.

Many have been damaged by the world, and wounded by the church.

The devil is laying traps for us.

Before the devil can catch us, he first baits the trap.

He knows what kind of bait to use.

He knows what kind of traps to use.

His job is to take you out by any means necessary.

Sickness and disease is at an all time high.

Many church folk are setting traps for us to fail.

So many of us are playing the blame game, but you can't allow stuff to cause you to lose your mind, or your faith.

You must learn your opponent in order to deal with him.

Many Christians are merely the devil's pawns to cause confusion in the body.

Confusion in the pulpit.

What doesn't kill you should make you stronger.

Many Christians have an assignment and the devil's purpose is to make your life a living hell.

It's not the sinners he is using.

It's these tongue talking people in the church that claim their Christians, but they are really assassins.

Many of you were molested and abused.

It was really meant to kill you.

Some were shot and stabbed.

It was really meant to kill you.

When God has a purpose for your life, it doesn't matter what you do or where you go, the devil is after you.

It's not you he wants; it's the seed that's been placed in you from birth.

It's going to cause you some pain, heartaches, and suffering for that seed to grow.

Don't allow yourself to be side tracked or to get caught up with manipulating people.

When you learn who you are, nobody can stop you.

When you know who you are, NO ONE can move you.

You must become like a tree planted by the rivers of water.

All of the hurt that you've been through in the church, was meant to kill you but God covered you.

The world and the church are full of influence where people have the power of persuasion over you.

They have learned how to control you and manipulate you without having your permission.

When you lose control over a situation, your mind gets invaded with all kinds of thoughts.

Like, "how did I get here?"

"What did I do to get here?"

"Is God angry with me?"

There are so many things we are fighting, so many things we are facing; but yet, many have no power over their flesh.

Could it be hurt from their past?

Or from the church?

It makes no difference.

Damaged is Damaged!

As we know, corrupt flesh causes you to die!

Sometimes spiritually, sometimes naturally.

Just like God is a spirit, the devil is a spirit and he listens to everything we say.

That's why you have to be careful of what you say, because the devil is waiting so that he can use it against you.

God wants you to live, but you have to die from gossiping, backbiting and fornicating.

I had to understand that pain is a teacher.

Don't let people know that they are affecting you.

Don't let them know that you are moved by what they are doing.

Every test that you go through should prepare you for your storm.

Your purpose and destiny is greater than your pain.

Sometimes in this Christian walk you will get wounded, but you have to get back into the fight.

Don't allow situations to make you stay home.

Don't abort your mission.

Finish what you have started.

Don't be overcome with evil, but overcome evil with good.

Many have so many wounds and scars from the world and the church. If you don't treat it, it will soon become infected, and then it will spread.

That's what's going on in the church.

We are trying to praise God with an open wound.

The more you seek God; he will begin to teach you survival tactics and how to employ them.

You have to stay away from people that always try to open up your wound with something negative.

Spreading through your body like a virus.

Sucking the life out of you! Because you are already broken.

One thing I learned while walking with God is, I found that storms are seasonal.

That means they come and go.

Since we are not capable of telling when they will come, we must be prepared.

Your mind must be in complete control of your body and your actions.

Don't be moved by what you don't have.

Sometimes storms destroy and sometimes they repay.

Sometimes God will send a major storm to catapult you into your destiny.

The more trials and suffering that you endure; you increase your net worth in the sight of God.

What are you worth to God?

For the bible says, "whatever is right, I'll pay".

You might be damaged now, but don't allow anyone else to kill your dreams because they can't see their way out!

People will plot against you just because you dream big. They will set traps for you to fall. Just like Joseph's brothers did all because of his dreams.

God gave me a word for the church in 2011.

"Those that have been faithful, those that have been obedient, those that have walked upright before Me, I will cause thee to flourish in everything that you do. The work you started shall and will be completed".

The Christians and preachers that have not been faithful, and have not walked upright before the Lord of Host shall be exposed, stricken with sickness, stripped of all of their wealth and prosperity.

Many will be exposed right on national television.

The spirit of Death shall hit many.

Those that have sought me with mind, heart and soul, despite of their weaknesses, shall be delivered.

A great famine is about to strike the land and only those of the household of Faith shall be spared, thus sayeth the Lord. "This is the time for the Apostles and Prophets. Not one word shall fall dead to the ground. For those that have touched my Prophets with their mouths and by the works of divination and witchcraft shall be punished. For I said in my Word, the Lord thy God shall do nothing except He first reveal His secret to his servant, the Prophet". *(Amos 3:7)*

Church is getting stagnated because there are too many babies in the church with grown up minds.

We can't handle anything, we can't take anything.

There is a copycat spirit in the church.

Whoever and what you hang around will become your DNA.

There are too many clones in the world and the church.

When you are different, you don't fit in.

When you are different, you are not easily accepted.

When you are different, you are excluded from certain things.

When you are different, people will find things to accuse you of, and assassinate your character, and slander your name.

I don't care if I don't fit in.

I want to be different.

I like being the odd ball, because I want to be like Christ.

I preached a message one day

"You're Gifted, but I'm Anointed".

The world and the church are full of gifted people.

In the world, we have psychics, mediums, witchcraft, and sorcery.

In the church we have prophecy and gifts of discerning. We are so gifted that we are out of control.

We don't care who we hurt in the process of trying to be great.

I don't want to be great; I just want to be heard.

It's time that we come from behind the pulpit and take it to the streets because the world is full of violence and chaos, murder and rape.

I have a question for you?

Who is qualified to save us, if we are all lying and killing each other?

While we are building buildings, who is building people?

Multimillion dollar facilities and half of the people in our ministry don't have a place to live.

As your pastor, I am responsible for you, because I am my brother's keeper.

And many will come that day and say Lord when have we saw you hungry, when have we saw you naked and thirsty, and he'll reply "*If you haven't done it unto me, you have done it unto the least of them*".

It's time for us to pull together as a people and stop fighting against each other and stop judging each other.

We are supposed to be Christ like; but if we are fighting in here, tell me who is fighting out there?

I don't know about you but it's time to take the city and kill the giants.

I believe drunks are tired of being drunks, prostitutes are tired of being prostitutes, and gang bangers are tired of being gang bangers.

It's time for us to get off of our seats of do nothing and go into the highways and hedges and compel them to come.

They want to come out but who is willing to go in?

We are losing our heritage, we are losing our sons and daughters, and we are losing our grand babies.

God said to me that we will never win the war against sin until we come together as a people.

There are so many churches that fast and pray and have shut INS but yet, they won't fellowship with you.

Something is wrong with that picture.

In fact, Satan is powerless.

The only power the devil has is what you give him.

It is a tactic that the devil is using to hinder you.

The reason his attacks are so fierce, is because he is afraid of what you will become.

So he can't afford to loosen his grip, and you can't afford to give up.

There are so many churches that don't believe in prophecy. It's being taught across America that you don't need a prophet to tell you anything.

Now, that is partially true.
When a prophet speaks he only comes to confirm, to warn, or expose.

That is one of the main reasons that prophesy is not accepted in the church. II Chronicles 20:20 says *and they rose early in the morning and went into the wilderness of Teko-a. And as they went forth, Jehoshaphat stood and said, here me, oh Judah, and ye inhabitants of Jerusalem, believe in the Lord your God, and so shall ye be established. Believe in His prophets and so shall ye prosper.*

Have you ever been in a place in your life where you were stuck, no growth, lost all desire to study your word, lost all of your desire to go to church, and to top it all off, there was never a person around to give you a word of encouragement.

So, you had to speak life into your own situation.

The church is dying, because it has been without a prophetic voice so long.

How can we accept so many gifts and the five fold ministry but reject prophecy?

Without all of the gifts operating in the church, the church becomes stagnated, unstable, out of control, because the five fold ministry comes to bring balance. *Ephesians 4:11* and *he gave some Apostles, some Prophets, some Evangelists, and some Pastors and Teachers for the perfecting of the saints for the work of the ministry, for the edifying of the body of Christ.*

I don't know about you, but I want every word that God's got for me prophetically.

My future depends on it!

Who's willing to be that voice of one crying in the wilderness, *prepare ye the way of the Lord*?

It's time to cry out loud and spare not. Lift up your voice as a trumpet and show my people their sins.

Church is dying... crying for help.

Crying out for attention and love.

But since most of the churches and Christians have a love problem, how can we expect to draw the sinners?

We can't produce what's not in us.

Because what's in you, is going to come out!

We've got to strive to live what we confess or we will become a liability instead of an asset.

The Church is being crippled by a judgmental spirit.

So if we are all so perfect and professing Christianity; where is the love?

The church has picked up a familiar spirit.

Many have become very critical and even pointing a finger when the bible says cast the mote and the beam out of your own eye first.

There was a time when we would really reverence God, but some of us are too anointed for God.

The bible says that there should only be One Lord, One Faith, and One baptism.

So where are all of these denominations coming from?

One faith is a belief.

Sinners chase the things of the world but, Christians seek after the things of God.

To me, suffering means to be without, to be broken.

Sometimes suffering alienates us from those who love us, because we don't know how to deal with our pain.

Sometimes pain is a trap.

When you're wounded you send out signals to those that feed on your pain.

Life is full of changes!

From a seed to a caterpillar, from a caterpillar to butterfly, from a butterfly to the sky.

Change is eminent.

It will happen in the course of time, but there is some shedding that must take place.

You must pull off things that don't belong, things that rob you of your joy, and things that make you sorrowful.

Choose your decisions wisely.

Anytime you have mixed emotions or second thoughts about-don't do it!

The devil's job is to get you so confused that you can't hear God.

Be careful of what you accept because everything is not of God.

When you're not healed, you can't handle the storms.

It is a conflict of interest to be caught between two lovers.

Relationship means commitment.

That means you come into accountability.

We all want the rewards and benefits of life but without a price. Without suffering, and lastly without being tested.

It is a proven fact that even in the economy; they will never put out a new product without testing its durability.

In other words, what is it made of?

Before your product is complete, and it reaches the world, it must go through a series of tests.

It takes time.

It takes commitment, and most of all, it takes patience.

There are several stages that you must go through, but the waiting will pay off.

In order to have a secure relationship with God, you must first confess your sins and be stripped of your independence, the way that you have been doing it.

In the growth process, God always sends you places that you don't want to go and to confront people that you don't want to deal with.

He will always give you things to say that you don't want to say.

Ask Moses.

We must understand that everything in life is a test to prove your loyalty to God.

In order to rain with God, we must suffer.

Those things that you don't understand and comprehend, he is making you comprehend and understand.

Everything that you go through in this life should teach you not to fall into the same pattern.

That's how the devil keeps tricking us.

We are falling in to the same pattern, dealing with the same stuff.

Surrounded by the same people and that's why you're getting the same results.

Relationships should be sentimental instead of temperamental.

Because you go to church, and speak in some kind of tongue, and prophesy and preach the Word of God, does not mean that you have a relationship with God.

For the bible says, many *"confess with their mouths but their heart are far from me"*.

Don't allow the devil to put fear in your heart that you can't fully commit.

If you can't afford to give up anything, how you can expect to receive anything, how can you handle what you've never released?

I want you to know that there is a shifting in the spirit.

Where many prophets and prophetesses are prophesying for fame and glory and not out of the mouth of God. *Jeremiah* 29:9 says *"for they prophesy falsely to you unto my name, I have not sent them saith the Lord".*

There is a difference between a gift and the anointing. Asks Hananiah. *"Then said the prophet Jeremiah unto Hananiah, the prophet, hear now hananiah the Lord hath not sent thee for thou maketh this people to trust in a lie. Therefore, thus saith the Lord, behold I will cast thee from the face of the earth, this year thou shalt die because thou has taught rebellion against the Lord. So Hananiah the prophet died the same year and the seventh month". (Jeremiah 28:15)*

God is tired of false prophets and preachers proclaiming blessings on those whom he has cursed.

There were times in my life when everything I tried to do failed.

It wasn't because God had left me, I was destined to die, but I was chosen to live.

There were times that even I felt like Jeremiah, the weeping prophet.

Not only was I crying, but I wanted to give up.

I begged God to let me die. He said, "you **are already dead. Now live"!**

I would speak prophetic words into other people's lives and it would come to pass, but yet I suffered.

I began to build up remorse and anger against God.

I lost everything.

I began to cry out like Job.

Because I didn't understand, for how I served God faithfully and He could forget about His servant.

He never answered me because it was destiny.

We were not created to be millionaires, have new houses, and drive new cars.

We were created to serve God.

How many people are we responsible for?

How many people have you wounded in the process of your deliverance?

Why do we keep offending each other?

I want to encourage everyone in ministry that have been through what I been through, but are still holding on, it is your destiny!

Don't think for one moment that God will allow you to have lived faithful on this earth and have you not reap a harvest.

It may not come from man. Man's got a way, but God's got a plan.

Tribulation should bring gratitude.

Biblical scholars and theologians would say that God will forgive you of any sin.

That's true!

But even God gets tired of repeat offenders.

Proverbs 1:24 says *"because I called and ye refused, I have stretched out my hand and no man regarded. But ye have set a naught all my council and would none of my reproof. I will also laugh at your calamity, I will mock when your fear comet h. When your fear comet h as a desolation and your destruction comet h as a whirlwind, when distress and anguish comet h upon you, then shall they call me. But I will not answer. They shall seek me early, but they shall not find me. For that they hated knowledge and did not choose to fear the Lord".*

In my early ministry, many mistakes were made.

By the age of thirty, I had been through four marriages.

I blamed a lot on my upbringing. I blamed it on my first wife after catching her in the bed with another man.

Can you imagine the devastation that my mind must have been going through?

The devil saw my wound and attacked!

I was powerless against the constant attacks.

Being raised without a father or mother, no schooling. I was searching for love from anyone that would give it to me.

Anyone that would listen.

It might have been wrong, but I refused to shack.

I was always a person that was full of passion and love but never knew what it felt like to receive it.

I became a prisoner in my own mind.

Wanting to post bail but no one would listen.

I prayed for death, but death would flee.

When I testified of what I had been through and how many times I had been married, the church and these fake preachers criticized me.

They said that I knew better.

God knows that I didn't.

I wanted to learn, but I had been called a failure all of my life, called mental, sick, reject, and stupid (even in ministry) and I started to believe it.

I've come to the conclusion that I was damaged by the world and wounded by the church.

Most of the time many Christians spend their time thinking about what others have done to them and where they are now.

As long as I kept contemplating, it was hard to see where I was going.

I had to learn how to stay in the storm without being affected by it.

The bible says "He will give you peace in the midst of your storm".

Storms come for two reasons... to make you quit or to build character.

(A word of encouragement) people will always see you fall, but they are not around when you get up.

Scars can easily heal, but as a dog licks his wounds after a fierce battle, we must treat our wounds in the midst of the fight.

Don't allow the devil to take the fight out of you.

The devil's greatest fear is that you will find out who you really are.

Here comes the devil again using my downfalls and bad marriages.

Ridicule from Christians and preachers, throwing my past up in my face to try to bring up homosexual tendencies after finding my wife in the bed with another man.

I said I would never deal with another woman.

The devil would send men my way to compliment me and say good things about me.

It seemed as though a woman was not around, but I thank God he kept me when I didn't have the strength to keep myself.

I thought all hope was lost.

Apparently, the relationship I thought I had with God never existed, because I built my relationship around what I thought people thought of me.

It affected my Christian walk.

I had to learn that one of the hardest things in life, is to go up against someone or something that you are not familiar with.

Immediately, it brings a spirit of inferiority.

You may be on the same common ground but you are unfamiliar with the tactics and strategy that they are using.

It's time that we become one step ahead of the enemy. If you are going to put your best man forward, make sure he can fight.

I had to come to the conclusion that your strength is not in the fighting, but what are you fighting for?

I've learned that sometimes anger will move you out of your fighting position.

Your strength is in your calmness. *"And I will keep you in perfect peace whose mind is stayed on me"*.

I want you to comprehend this:

The things that oppress you, and constantly hinder you, are things you might be aware of but don't know its motive.

To know a things motive, is to have insight in time.

To be oppressed and depressed is a spirit that the devil uses as his main weapon.

He will force you into a fight without having time to prepare.

So instead of standing still, you take the bait, causing you to commit sin without thinking about the consequences.

The fear is in what you do not know and what you have not seen.

I have learned that preparation is in training.

I must have good wind, because the battle could be longer than we anticipate.

So you must keep on fighting even when you are tired.

My eyesight must also be sharp so that I can see the traps from a distance.

The problem with us facing our giants, is we get caught up in what we see.

The word "prepare" means to make preparation.

You will never experience victory without preparation.

Who and what we give our allegiance to becomes our master, and we become its slave.

In order to be free, you must first find out what causes you to serve that giant in your life.

(How can one fight unless he or she is aware of what they are dealing with?)

When we move in our flesh, we disable the shield of protection.

Now you're fighting without a covering.

You've got to take the chastisement.

You've got to take the constructive criticism.

Sometimes you've got to walk alone to become strong.

That's real!

You're purpose is what propels you to the next level.

When your purpose is being revealed to you, the devil begins to counter attack with the lust of your flesh.

I had to learn that God will give you power over your enemies while they are resting. Ask Joshua.

You need to learn how to take advantage of the times that God is granting you peace.

The greatest survival tactic in war is not food, it's your endurance.

Which is your will to live?

(Until we learn how to see us, for who we are, we will never see Him for who He is).

When we are not focused, we keep falling into traps that were not even meant for us.

The more carnal you are, the weaker you become.

When we are not prayed up, the slightest thing will offend us.

We have to learn to grow and mature beyond our understanding.

Many of our hurts have come from things we have chased and pursued that God did not call us to.

Many times we fall.

It's simply because we have not taken the necessary precautions.

I've come to the conclusion that only the strong will survive.

Everything in life that is weak doesn't last long.

When there are weak moments in your life, when there is silence instead of praise, it becomes easy to be deceived.

A lying spirit has infiltrated the church and those that are weak are sucked right in.

In order to be Christ like, it's going to cost you something.

Sometimes it's something that you don't want to give.

Your prayer must be urgent.

Your praise must become overwhelming and your worship but becomes UN-ordinary.

I don't know about you, but I don't mind being in spiritual labor just as long as I have this baby.

So many Christians are having spiritual miscarriages.

Aborting their destiny.

It's because they can't deal with the pain of what God chose them to carry.

Sometimes it's hard to conceive a life when you have no life.

You don't have time to doubt!

That's a spiritual seed you have been pregnant with for some time.

Even though you are going through your pregnancy right now, your pregnancy is not a mistake!

You need to tell the devil that "I am going to have this baby, even if it kills me!"

Tell God, "My faith needs to be restored and the only hope that I have left is in what I have, and it's not enough to sustain me. Lord get me out of this thing and get this thing out of me! Even though I lack the faith, don't let me lose my trust. For it is in you that I move and have my being. "

Jesus didn't receive his breakthrough until he died on the cross and rose again.

Now all we have to do is die to the flesh and the more you die, your thirst begins to change. *"For they that thirst after righteousness shall be filled"*.

It is indigenous to believe otherwise that he will do exactly what he says.

When you allow yourself to fall in a trap, you must learn how to escape.

Sometimes the only way to escape is to break out in a crazy praise.

You see a person who is crazy and no one wants to hang around.

Your praise has to become just like that!

When your mind tells you no, so should your body!

But since you don't have power over your mind, your body will refuse to submit.

The pain that you are suffering is most likely due to your stubbornness.

One thing I had to learn about wounds is that sometimes they don't easily heal.

Especially when you are damaged in the church.

Depending on how deep the wound is, will determine how long it will take you to recover.

The devil uses things that you have been through to reopen old wounds.

As Christians, we must understand that there is a price on our head.

The devil is not going to just lie down and allow you to be blessed.

His job is to cause constant pressure so that you can curse God.

When you curse God, you have cursed your season.

Be careful when you are going through this of who you get hooked up with, because some things are a trap.

There is an increase in the spirit of want in the church and the world.

Everybody is looking for something or somebody.

The Army is looking for a few good men and the world is looking for anything that they can get their hands on.

Some of your wants and desires have caused you to forsake God.

In order for us to grasp the fundamentals and the simplicity of God, we must learn to be a hearer and a doer of the Word.

The church has turned into a sideshow.

It's hard to tell the real from the fake.

Unless we learn how to sell out, we will remain vegetarians because we won't eat the meat.

It's hard to sell out because what's in you don't want to come out.

So God has to castrate you from yourself.

When you're sold out, nothing matters.

When you're going through this, things will be detected, but you won't be affected.

The things that you love the most are keeping you from true worship.

Because you keep praising God for what he's done for you and you never got into worship.

Because until you sell out, you will never worship.

I want you to know that it hurts when you lose things, but things can be replaced.

The anointing can't.

The world is seeking direction, but can't get it because they don't trust the church.

It's time to stop worrying about the things you have no power to change.

Real deliverance will never take place in the church, until we put our titles down.

The anointing causes controversy, and the love of money causes scandals.

It's not the church that's really got a bad name; it's the people in the church.

They are using Gods name to gain recognition, in the sight of people.

Many churches are trapped in a zone of believing quantity is better than quality.

The church has lost respect for each other we don't care how we talk to each other.

Many leaders have people in positions that are unclean, just to say you have a full staff.

We the people must come to the conclusion that we are responsible for each other.

The Bible says you are your brother's keeper and how can you have my back when you've got your foot on my neck and my name in your mouth?

The church has turn into one big side freak show.

Many people go to church looking for the anointing and end up getting entertained.

It is evident that this is not the church He died for.

If it were why is he judging it first.

Whoever we allow to operate in the church that is unclean will cause a wondering spirit to roam free in the church looking for a victim that's weaker than where it came out of.

The Bible says when an unclean spirit is gone out of a man, he looks for dry places.

He then brings seven more spirits worse than before.

The church has lost its identity due to hidden agendas.

We try to imitate each other because we don't possess the ability to pursue our own anointing so we end up becoming counterfeits. *It is a sad case and shame before God* that we are so anointed that we can't see our own mistakes so we spend all day pointing out everybody else's.

Even the court system says, "I am innocent until proven guilty" but all the church has to do is get wind of it, without even giving you a chance to have a trial of jurors, and immediately the killing starts.

They don't won't to wound you for your mistakes they want you to have the electric chair.

This is a word for the preachers that have taken possession of the church,

God wants his church back.

If we are who we say we are, then why is he judging us first?

Counterfeit Christianity produces judgment.

When someone is telling us the truth we attack them.

I have come to the conclusion that church and politics don't mix.

The church is being run like a business, but what about the people

That don't fit in to what you want to do any and everything goes!

We fire people from position because someone else is a better tither, or we just want somebody to be our due boy, perhaps you can't comprehend the word due boy, in the modern vernacular world, it means flunky.

God is judging the church first, and in case you didn't know, that means you.

Who have you been lying on, who have you miss-treated?

Who are you backbiting against?

What other pastors have you had meetings on?

Before I got really delivered I used to be a controlling Pastor.

Telling Gods people that wanted to leave the ministry that I'm not going to release you.

God told me you didn't die for him.

Many modern day preachers have become Jim Jones, a modern-day Pharaoh.

The church has become so political to the point that we rarely see miracles happening.

What sense does it make to be popular with men but out of line with God?

Many have gotten caught up in money and fame and lost their mantle.

There are too many people that have been wounded by the church that have become outcast because of their past.

Many have gone back to the world because of the attacks from the church from the pulpit, from the media and most of all from those they love.

What is the solution to this madness we call church?

Is there a solution?

Who has a remedy?

I never thought I'd ever see a time when another pastor would tell me to send a CD or tape.

I thought the bible said to know them that labor among you?

It's time that may begin to seek the face of God and forget about being popular, forget about being on television, forget about being recognized, it's not about building a mega-ministry! and its focus on building God's people taking gods people to the next level.

Allowing God's people to be healed in deliverance services.

The church has become one big fashion show.

Many pastors are crying out to God for change, not allowing Gods people to go visit other ministries.

I had to learn the hard way that I'm not the only pastor that God called, I am not the only pastor that God anointed, God will send people to us for season and when it seasons up we have to release for the bible teaches us that they are different diversities of gifts but the same spirit we gleam from each other we learn from each other, but how can I learn from you if you're too good for me?

How can I learn from you if you won't fellowship with me?

Because I am not on their level and because I don't have a mega-ministry, they would not connect with me... for twenty three years of pastoring it has been lonely for me crying out, looking for a spiritual father, but instead, I ran into a brick wall. In the end I found out they did not want to be connected and God did not want me to connect with them..

Those of you that have experienced what I've experienced, this is your time. Those of you that did not bow to bail ,God is about to grant you the keys to everything that has been locked up, everything that has been hidden , and not revealed is about to come into fruition.

This is your last year, your last moment of silence, which seems as if no one cares, no ones concerned, no one hears you, no one understands you and no one responds... but God heard you the first time, you have passed the test you would never walk alone again, this is your hour of release , you haven't given yourself over to money you have not given yourself over to lust, sex or pride, or perversion, you have waited on me and now is your time.

Don't worry about being an outcast because everyone is the son of God.

A warning from the prophet and a warning from God, "those that have used the Lord's name in vain, those that have built wealth and prosperity using the Lord's name in vain, you are about to be exposed, you will be exposed.

Real Christians don't gossip, real Christians are not busy bodies in other man's matters, real Christians don't slander each others name.

Real pastors fellowship with everybody, real pastors are not stand offish real pastors take their phone calls because they want to be connected to other men and women of God, what is God saying about us? will the real pastors and Christian please stand up?

We are losing the war trying to be seen without losing the war trying to be wealthy, who is qualified to save us?

Who can I trust that would not condemn me as a pastor, as a Christian? because of my mistakes even the woman that was caught in the act of adultery, Jesus told them "He without sin cast the first stone", they dropped their heads and walked away because they all had sinned..

The Bible says "To him that says he has no sin he is a liar and the truth is not in him" the Bible also says "He that cover of his sins will not prosper", so I am no better than you and you are no better than me.

Where is the love in the church ? this is not the church he died for.

Damaged by the world and wounded by the church

The church is suffering from darkness, it is to be destitute of light and not radiating or reflecting light.

Wholly or partially black having the quality opposite to white and a state of being gloomy or to concealed, which means to cover up.

Secretive, mysterious, to deprive light, For open vision.

To be in darkness means we struggle with the change that God uses to invoke light.

To be in darkness means there is void that produces light and because of what I see. I can visualize.

So it is impossible to see in the dark.

The Bible says in John 3:19 "this the condemnation that light is come into the world, and men loved the world rather than light, because these deeds were evil."

As Christians if we are not careful we can get caught up in darkness, and as we continue to articulate the practice of sin, we enter into gross darkness.

Darkness is one of the most effective weapons the devil uses to infiltrate light, to keep you from seeing.

Being in darkness causes us not to love one another.

Being in gross darkness causes us to hate one another.

Most of the time darkness is formulated around sin.

For Christians, the Bible says to walk in the light and you will not fulfill the lust of the flesh.

Darkness is centered around pain, most of the things that are tragic happens at night, because the devil knows that his chances of conquering are few.

So he uses the gross darkness to emanate his power, because light and darkness has no fellowship, that's why we must choose one.

Because of sin, darkness is sweeping through the church, controlling our leaders, blinding us from our deliverance, and because of darkness, we fight against each other, because of darkness.

We judge each other, the spirit of darkness is over powering our church and because of darkness, God is judging the church first.

The light represents the truth and the truth shall make you free, for the wages of sin is death.

One thing I learned about death, is that it has many names, but no face, it doesn't care who it kills or who it hurts.

Damaged by the world and wounded by the church.

God told me when you write this book "I don't want another sequel, or another novel".

The people need to hear a word from God, and not from the passion of my heart. Our words carry no change when we don't posses the spirit of God, and that's why people can read our books and there is no deliverance. The church has turned into a harlot, and if you don't know the term, it means whore. Many leaders and Christian's are willing to do what ever it takes to survive, just to get their needs met.

Gods not looking for motivated speaker's, elegant teachers, but soul reacher's.

Here's the funny thing... we argue about whose anointed, we debate on national TV, we kill each other, and you wonder why he is judging the church first?

Many pastors, apostles and bishops, when God led me to speak in to there lives, they became notable and the prophecy came to pass, and they forgot about me ...some are now on TBN, some are now on word network, some have their own TV network.

I want to personally encourage every pastor, that has spent time with other leaders investing in other leaders.

But there is another group of pastors I want to talk about. Once they became recognized they put you on the back burner, like you were nothing.

Don't worry you will not leave this earth without reaping your harvest. God is making way for every Joshua! Many of you have been looking for a spiritual father, but most of them are to busy... even God makes time for me, they never return your calls. You can always tell who the self made pastors and preachers are, they don't want to fellowship, when the bible says to show yourself friendly. They always judge other pastors, when the bible says to restore such a one in the spirit of meekness considering yourself. The bible also says to testify to that- that you know, and have seen. Damaged by the world and wounded by the church. The problem with the church is leadership, will the real pastors please stand up. It is time that we take the church back through prayer, we are not going to get the church back through competition. We are not going to get the church back threw the spirit of control. As we read in the book of Jeremiah 23 "woe be onto the pastors who scatter the sheep of my pasture", whose sheep? Gods. In that same passage it says that God will gather up the remnant of his flock out of all countries weather God himself have driven them away, and he said "he would set up other Shepard over them and they will fear no more nether shall there be any lacking". The church has become victimize by control, abuse, witchcraft, jealousy, money laundering, Lesbian homosexuality . If we stop building buildings and build people, maybe God would change the verdict of judging the church first. Many have compromised for a book, compromised to get on TV, at what price are you willing to sell your soul for.

If I were you, I would stop passing judgment, if I were you I would I would try to fellowship with every body! The bible says "let the wheat and the tare grow together and God would do the separating". So who are you to say whose not right. Even God uses handicapped people to do extraordinary things. (I'm praying for your forgiveness father please forgive me), I have lived a hypocritical life, I have misused your pulpit for my private battle ground I have pushed other pastors and Christians away because of what some one else said about them. Forgive me for using my gift to hurt people, forgive me for having a spirit of control as a pastor. Telling your people I'm not going to release you when you release me when your son died for me. Let your people go your last warning. No time for competition who has the most members? Whose church is larger? Whose on what network? Where is God in all of this? Damaged by the world and wounded by the church.

If you would like to contact me about this book
drlee712@yahoo.com
www.Williamleeministries.org

Personal Note from Sandra:

I was raised by my parents. My dad was a preacher.
I spent many years in search of a church that I felt at
home in.
I didn't find it.

All of these years I have searched, been thirsty,
hungry for the Lord. Praying faithfully and believing
that I was satisfied with loving God right here at
home.
Then, I met Apostle William D Lee and Evangelist
Anita Wilson and my heart found God's word, and his
love and patience. I truly *feel* God through these
people. Let this be a season of apologies, repentance,
and forgiveness.

CPSIA information can be obtained at www.ICGtesting.com
Printed in the USA
BVOW10s2136091013

333377BV00007B/52/P